MW00783784

WITHDRAWN

EELS

LIVING WILD

Published by Creative Education and Creative Paperbacks
P.O. Box 227, Mankato, Minnesota 56002
Creative Education and Creative Paperbacks are imprints of The Creative Company
www.thecreativecompany.us

Design and production by Mary Herrmann
Art direction by Rita Marshall
Printed in China

Photographs by Creative Commons Wikimedia (Brocken Inaglory, Ratha Grimes/ Flickr, Gusmonkeyboy, Hans Hillewaert, Roban Kramer/Flickr, NOAA Photo Library/Flickr, Pseudonpanax, Stan Shebs, MelissaMStewart, Chika Watanabe/Flickr), Deviant Art (vbljyjxtdf), Dreamstime (Rafael Ben Ari, Galinasavina), Flickr (Andrew David/NOAA/NMFS/SEFSC Panama City and Lance Horn/UNCW/NURC – Phantom II ROV operator/NOAA Photo Library, NOAA OKEANOS Explorer Program/2013 Northeast U.S. Canyons Expedition/NOAA Photo Library, Vailulu'u 2005 Exploration/NOAA-OE/NOAA Photo Library), Getty Images (DEA PICTURE LIBRARY/De Agostini, Borut Furlan/WaterFrame), iStockphoto (segawa7, Shur_ ca, swissmediavision, InesWiehle), NOAA (Ocean Explorer; SEFSC Pascagoula Laboratory/Collection of Brandi Noble, NOAA/NMFS/SEFSC), Shutterstock (Bety X, Kim Briers, John Brueske, Chris Button, Rich Carey, Chaikom, Jung Hsuan, Ellen Hui, THANEESA INTHARAWICHAI, Katerinina, Adam Ke, Irina Kozorog, LagunaticPhoto, MJUP, nartt, Natursports, mario pesce, Katsiaryna Pleshakova, Nicolas Primola, scubaluna, Vlad61, Richard Whitcombe, zaferkizilkaya)

Copyright © 2019 Creative Education, Creative Paperbacks
International copyright reserved in all countries. No part of this book may be reproduced in any form without written permission from the publisher.

Library of Congress Cataloging-in-Publication Data
Names: Gish, Melissa, author.
Title: Eels / Melissa Gish.
Series: Living wild.
Includes index.
Summary: A look at eels, including their habitats, physical characteristics such as their elongated bodies, behaviors, relationships with humans, and the migratory spawning of some freshwater species in the world today.
Identifiers: LCCN 2017035414 / ISBN 978-1-60818-957-1 (hardcover) / ISBN 978-1-62832-562-1 (pbk) / ISBN 978-1-64000-036-0 (eBook)

Subjects: LCSH: Eels—Juvenile literature.
Classification: LCC QL637.9.A5 G57 2018 / DDC 597/.43—dc23

CCSS: RI.5.1, 2, 3, 8; RST.6-8.1, 2, 5, 6, 8; RH.6-8.3, 4, 5, 6, 7, 8

First Edition HC 9 8 7 6 5 4 3 2 1
First Edition PBK 9 8 7 6 5 4 3 2 1

CREATIVE EDUCATION • CREATIVE PAPERBACKS

EELS

Melissa Gish

The morning sun warms the clear blue waters of a coral reef, coaxing a juvenile zebra moray

eel from its hiding place. It glides through the water, weaving among sea fans and anemones.

T the morning sun warms the clear blue waters of a coral reef, coaxing a juvenile zebra moray eel from its hiding place. It glides through the water, weaving among sea fans and anemones. Here in Hawaii's vast Papahānaumokuākea (*pa-pa-HAH-no-MO-koo-ah-KAY-uh*) Marine National Monument, wildlife is abundant. The zebra moray eel swims toward the seabed, scanning for movement. Suddenly, the sand shifts, revealing a green swimming crab. The moray eel darts

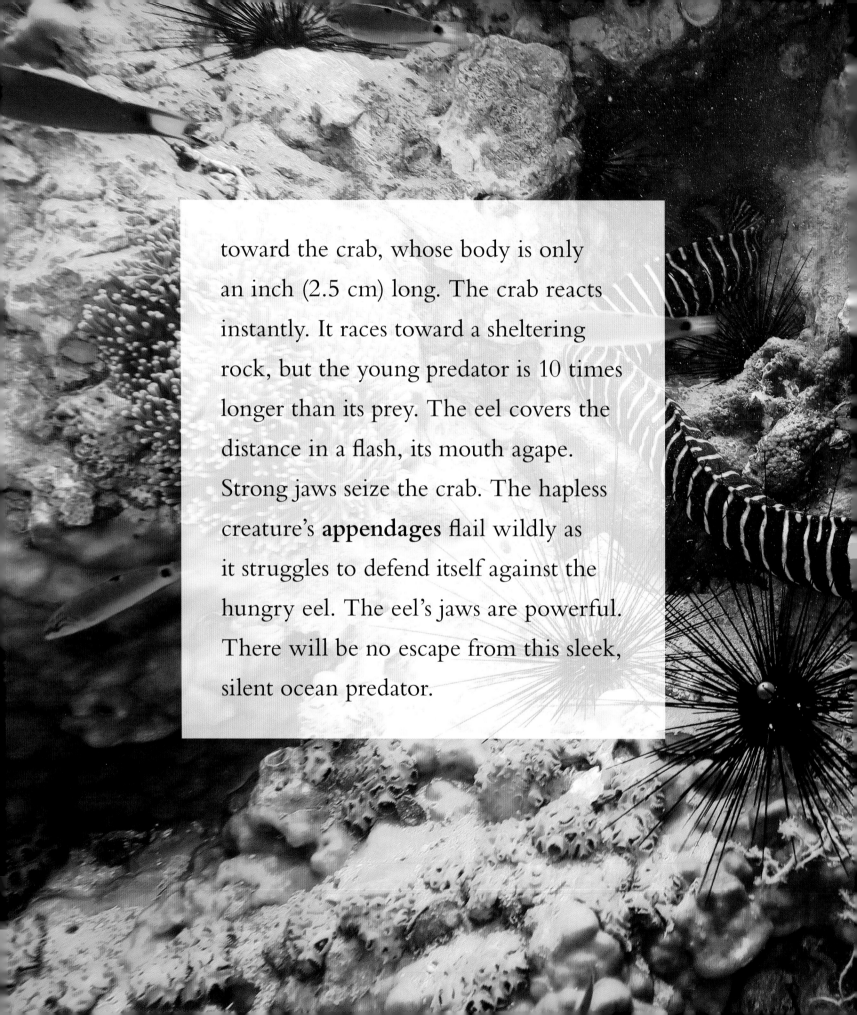

toward the crab, whose body is only
an inch (2.5 cm) long. The crab reacts
instantly. It races toward a sheltering
rock, but the young predator is 10 times
longer than its prey. The eel covers the
distance in a flash, its mouth agape.
Strong jaws seize the crab. The hapless
creature's **appendages** flail wildly as
it struggles to defend itself against the
hungry eel. The eel's jaws are powerful.
There will be no escape from this sleek,
silent ocean predator.

WHERE IN THE WORLD THEY LIVE

Freckled Pike Conger
Gulf of Mexico and the northern coast of South America from Colombia to French Guiana

New Zealand Longfin Eel
New Zealand

Sharptail Eel
coastal western Atlantic from southern Florida to southern Brazil

Ocellated Moray Eel
coastal waters of the U.S. East Coast and the Gulf of Mexico

Lesser Sand Eel
northeastern Atlantic from Portugal to southern Iceland and western Russia

Ribbon Moray Eel
coastal waters of Southeast Asia and Oceania

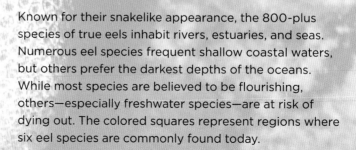

Known for their snakelike appearance, the 800-plus species of true eels inhabit rivers, estuaries, and seas. Numerous eel species frequent shallow coastal waters, but others prefer the darkest depths of the oceans. While most species are believed to be flourishing, others—especially freshwater species—are at risk of dying out. The colored squares represent regions where six eel species are commonly found today.

AN ENDLESS ARRAY OF EELS

The lesser spiny eel is a shy freshwater eel from Southeast Asia that grows to a length of about 14 inches (35.6 cm).

Eels are a kind of fish with an elongated, snakelike body, pointed head, and long jaws. Eels do not chew food. They swallow it whole. Most have sharp, backward-pointing teeth. Eels may shake or spin to rip off chunks of meat from larger meals. Powerful muscles push food down the throat. Some eels, such as zebra moray and whitemouthed moray eels, have flat teeth used for crushing shellfish. Freshwater eels have tiny scales embedded in their skin. Other eels have smooth, rubbery skin. Eels can be one solid color or have striking spots, stripes, zigzags, and blotches. Glands in the skin produce **mucus**. This slimy substance helps eels glide through the water with little resistance and protects the eels' skin from scrapes and cuts as they maneuver around rocks and other solid objects. Some eels are able to line their sandy or rocky burrows with mucus for further protection. A few species, including the daggertooth pike conger eel, have mucus that contains deadly poison.

Like all fish, eels breathe through slits in their bodies called gills. As eels swim, water is forced over the gills,

Adult male ribbon morays are blue with a yellow mouth and dorsal fin, while adult females are all yellow.

where thin **membranes** collect oxygen and transfer it to the eel's bloodstream. When eels are not swimming, they open and close their mouths to pump water over their gills. Eels have a pair of pectoral fins behind the gills. Some have a dorsal (back) fin, caudal (tail) fin, and anal (underside) fin that are all connected. This continuous, ribbonlike fin runs almost the entire length of the eel's body. Some eels have only pectoral fins, and others have no fins at all. Eels swim by moving their bodies in a wavelike motion. This is similar to how snakes move on land. Most eels can swim about two miles (3.2 km) per hour. The average human can swim nearly twice as fast.

Eels are preyed upon by a variety of fish, including sharks, barracudas, and groupers, as well as sea kraits, which are venomous sea snakes. Eels typically hide under rock ledges, in caves and crevices, or in mud or patches of **aquatic** plants. Hidden from view, they can be safe, but they also poise themselves to ambush passing prey. Eels have poor eyesight, so they rely on their powerful sense of smell to locate prey. Many eels have nostrils that extend outward from their snouts. Some nostrils are wormlike or

The starry moray, also known as the yellowmouth moray, pumps water through its gills as it waits for prey.

The leopard moray, also known as the dragon moray, has long, tubular nostrils and projections above the eyes for detecting prey.

frilly. These are used to lure prey closer. Depending on the species, eels may feed on smaller fish, worms, frogs, aquatic birds, **crustaceans**, fish eggs, **zooplankton**, and dead animals.

Eels belong to the order Anguilliformes. This name comes from the Latin *anguis*, which means "snake," and *forma*, which means "the form of." The more than 800 different eel species vary greatly in both size and color. Most live in saltwater habitats. Only 18 species live in fresh water. Anguilliformes is divided into four suborders based on anatomy and **genetics**. One suborder is made up of sawtooth and snipe eels. Sawtooth eels get their name from the shape of their inward-slanting teeth that are attached to a bone in the roof of the mouth. Snipe eels have a unique jaw that looks like the long, slender beak of a wading bird called a snipe. Most sawtooth eels grow to about 12 inches (30.5 cm). Long and thin, snipe eels can reach 6.5 feet (2 m). These eels live in the deep ocean.

A second suborder contains cutthroat eels. These eels typically remain on the seafloor and have been found more than two miles (3.2 km) deep. They vary in length

Once prey has entered a moray eel's mouth and been snagged by the inner jaws, escape is impossible.

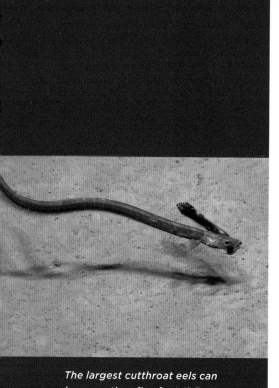

The largest cutthroat eels can be more than five feet (1.5 m) long and dive more than two miles (3.2 km) deep.

The Ingolf duckbill eel uses the spatula-like tip on its snout to plow through sand in search of crustaceans.

from about nine inches (22.9 cm) to more than five feet (1.5 m). Conger eels and their closest kin make up the third suborder. Congers are some of the largest eels. In 2015, British fisherman Scott Govier hauled in a 7-foot-long (2.1 m) European conger eel that weighed 131 pounds (59.4 kg). It was just two pounds (0.9 kg) shy of a 1995 record catch. These are unusual cases, though. Most of the 180 conger eel species are less than 7 feet (2.1 m) long. Within the conger suborder are garden eels, which get their name from their unique behavior of sticking straight up like plant stalks from burrows in the seabed. Other conger families include snake eels, which lack fins and have blunt snouts, allowing them to easily burrow into soft mud. And longneck eels have slender necks with stripes on the head that connect to sensory organs, while bottom-dwelling duckbill eels have long, flat snouts that look like ducks' bills.

The fourth suborder contains the eels with which people are most familiar as well as some recently discovered species. Freshwater eels are found in rivers, lakes, and **estuaries** around the world. This group includes the European, Japanese, and American eels.

Garden eels tend to live in groups, which makes them look even more like plants "growing" in a garden.

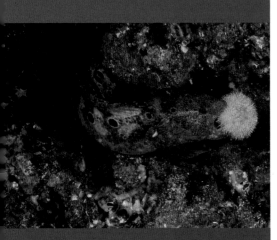

Although not a true eel, the wolf eel is called that because of its body shape, which is similar to its relatives'.

The giant moray can weigh up to 66 pounds (29.9 kg), and the New Zealand longfin eel can weigh nearly 90 pounds (40.8 kg).

Morays are saltwater eels that are typically the most colorful. The more than 200 moray species vary greatly in size. The Snyder's moray, the world's smallest moray eel, grows to just 4.5 inches (11.4 cm) long. On the other end of the spectrum is the slender giant moray. It can grow to 13 feet (4 m). Morays are also the only fish known to possess a second jaw structure, called a pharyngeal jaw, in the throat. This set of jaws can thrust upward from the throat to grab prey and drag it into the eel's **gullet**. Also in this suborder are false morays, which tend to be smaller than true morays. False morays range from about 6 to 16 inches (15.2–40.6 cm) in length. Other eels in this suborder include mud eels, which are burrowers, and spaghetti eels, which are named for their long, slender bodies. Thin eels are a rarely seen deep-sea species that have been studied only since the 1990s. And in 2009, the Palauan primitive cave eel was discovered in waters off the Republic of Palau, east of the Philippines. Scientists called this eel "primitive" because it has many of the characteristics of prehistoric eels seen in fossils from the Cretaceous period of more than 100 million years ago.

The giant moray contributes to the health of its seabed habitat by feeding on weak crustaceans, fish, and octopuses.

Conger eels have oval-shaped eyes that are much larger than the rounded eyes of most other eel species.

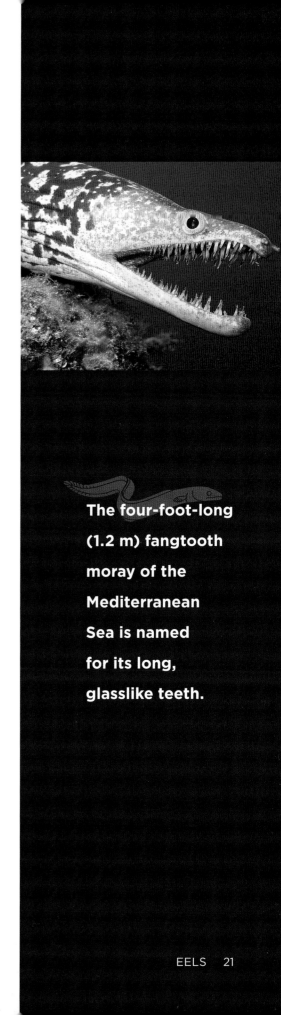

M ost eels are shy and nocturnal, hiding during the day and hunting at night. Eels are not social animals, but many species find safety in numbers. Swaths of garden eels may cover the seabed, and white-eyed morays may gather in swarms of 30 or 40 under ledges of coral reefs. Some moray eels, such as speckled, giant, and yellow morays, defend a territory against intruders. Territorial eels will tolerate other fish––including other moray species––in their cave or crevice, but they will chase away invading morays of their own kind. These eels may even engage in biting battles to defend their homes. For a long time, people believed morays were dangerous, but this has been proven false. Despite their shyness, most moray eels are also curious. They typically do not flee from human divers but rather seem to watch the strangers in their habitat. They may even approach divers, cautiously encircling them to get a closer look. This can be unnerving to divers who are unaccustomed to being so close to a nine-foot-long (2.7 m) fish capable of gulping down a person's entire arm. However, morays do not bite unless they are provoked or feel cornered. Captive morays even appear to remember

The four-foot-long (1.2 m) fangtooth moray of the Mediterranean Sea is named for its long, glasslike teeth.

Young morays are vulnerable in the vast ocean and must rely on camouflage to hide from predators.

Many eel species are sequential hermaphrodites, which means they are one gender as larvae and then change to a different gender.

familiar divers. The eels playfully interact with the divers, rubbing against them and turning on their sides to be petted.

Eels have one of the most remarkable life cycles in the animal kingdom—and one of the least understood. Scientists do not know where most eel species reproduce, where the eggs are laid, or how newly hatched eels survive. What scientists do know is that eels reproduce just once. The female lays eggs, the male fertilizes them, and then the parent eels die. The offspring are left to develop and survive completely on their own. When eels first hatch, they are **larvae** called leptocephali, which means "small head." They are transparent, and their flat bodies are shaped like the leaves of a willow tree. Leptocephali have long teeth, and most species have big eyes. Depending on the species, they range from less than 2 to nearly 12 inches (5.1–30.5 cm) long. The hatching of eel larvae has rarely been witnessed in the wild, and **captive-breeding** has met with little success. In 2004, after decades of research, Japanese scientists were able to hatch freshwater Japanese eels, but most of the larvae died. Those that survived were deformed. Ten years later, two ribbon morays at Schönbrunn Zoo in Vienna, Austria, spawned, and their eggs hatched. It was the first time in

history a moray eel species hatched in captivity, but the larvae survived for only one week.

As eel larvae grow, their bodies become slender and round. The long teeth are replaced by shorter ones. This process can take up to a year. At the end of this stage, they are called glass eels. Their eyes are two black spots at the head of a transparent body. Some species are no thicker than a strand of hair. Eels that are captured from the wild at this stage can be kept alive in captivity. No one knows what glass eels eat in the wild, but in captivity, they are fed liquefied fish. As the glass eels develop, they grow larger and darker. When they are no longer transparent, they are called elvers. Depending on the

Juvenile ribbon eels of both genders are black with yellow dorsal fins until they reach maturity.

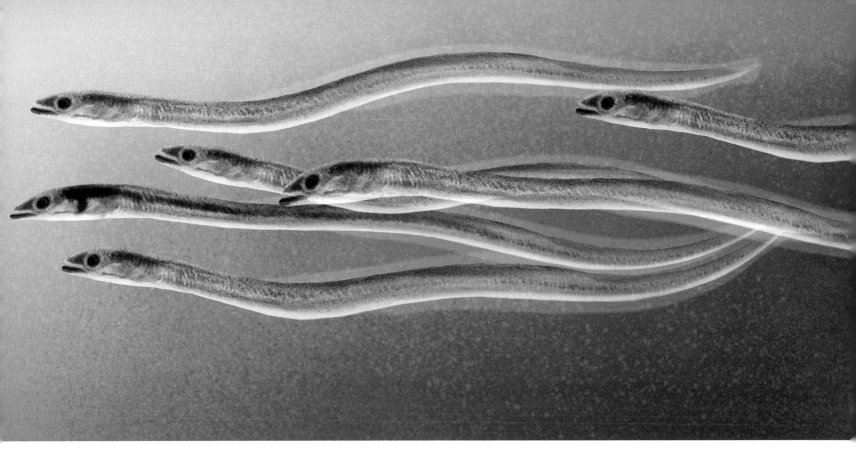

Concerned about the overfishing of elvers in U.S. rivers, conservationists have proposed stronger laws to protect them.

species, elvers can be 4 to 24 inches (10.2–61 cm) long. Growth to adult size takes anywhere from 3 to 40 years. If they do not reproduce, many eel species can live to be 60 years old. New Zealand longfin eels are known to live 100 years. Unproven stories of older eels have made their way into the news. A Swedish farmer reported that his family had kept a European freshwater eel in a well for three generations. He said the eel was 155 years old when it died in 2014. Dr. Håkan Wickström, a scientist at the Swedish University of Agricultural Sciences, reported that it was quite possible for the eel to have lived that long in a safe environment with plenty of food, though no one knows for sure how long eels can live.

As if the eel's life cycle was not already radically different enough, freshwater eels of North America and Europe take their reproductive process even farther—up to 4,000 miles (6,437 km) farther! Most freshwater eels are catadromous, which means they are hatched in salt water, travel to fresh water for their adult lives, and then return to the sea to reproduce. How eels know when to spawn is another mystery. Every autumn, when individual American and European freshwater eels sense they have reached an appropriate age, they travel together to the Sargasso Sea. Some may be just a few years old, while others may be 20. The Sargasso Sea is a vast body of warm water in the middle of the cold Atlantic. It is covered with huge patches of free-floating seaweed called sargassum, which gives this "ocean within an ocean" its name. Instead of land borders, the Sargasso Sea is bounded by ocean currents: the North Atlantic Current to the north, the Canary Current to the east, the North Atlantic Equatorial Current to the south, and the Gulf Stream to the west. The weather in the Sargasso Sea is always calm and warm. It is the perfect habitat for eels—and many other ocean species such as sea turtles and porbeagle sharks—to begin their lives.

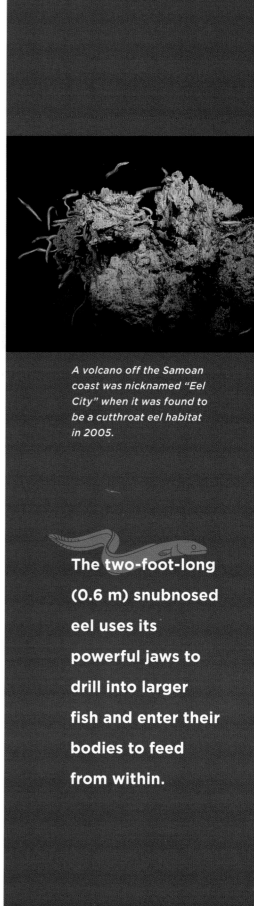

A volcano off the Samoan coast was nicknamed "Eel City" when it was found to be a cutthroat eel habitat in 2005.

The two-foot-long (0.6 m) snubnosed eel uses its powerful jaws to drill into larger fish and enter their bodies to feed from within.

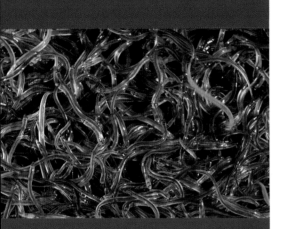

Scientists are still struggling to unravel the mysteries surrounding the diet and development of glass eels in the wild.

After hatching, the leptocephali do not stay in the Sargasso Sea. They begin drifting northward, starting a journey that takes about a year. Then, as glass eels, they make their way to the mouths of rivers on North America's eastern coast and Europe's western shores. Their bodies **adapt** to the fresh water, and they swim inland, where they transform into elvers. After one more year, they reach adult size and are called yellow eels, a name they get from their yellowish-green color. Freshwater eels can live for decades in lakes, rivers, ponds, and streams—sometimes alone and sometimes in swarms. When instinct sparks them to reproduce, the eels eat until they have nearly 30 percent body fat. Not all freshwater eels reproduce, but those that do return to coastal estuaries, where they readapt to saltwater conditions. Their eyes and pectoral fins get bigger, and their skin thickens. They turn bluish with white bellies. Now called silver eels, they head out to sea. The eels do not eat again for the rest of their lives. No one knows exactly when or where in the Sargasso Sea these eels spawn, because no one has ever been able to track them. It is one of science's greatest mysteries.

Freshwater eels are a welcome predator in North America's Lake Ontario, where they feed on the nonnative round goby.

Now housed in the National Roman Museum, a fresco from the second century A.D. depicts a fight between a moray eel, a lobster, and an octopus.

GUARDIANS, PEACEMAKERS, AND MONSTERS

I n ancient times, eels were viewed with great respect. In about 450 B.C., an eel **cult** arose in Egypt. Eels were kept in ponds and fed soft animal guts. Followers believed that eels were symbolic of new life and held the power of the sun in their shimmering bodies. In the fourth century B.C., people in Greece believed that the god Zeus used eels to carry rainwater to the ground. Eels were also considered one of the finest delicacies in ancient times. The government of Sybaris, Sicily, collected no tax from eel fishermen, because providing eels was considered a public service. Publius Vedius Pollio was a Roman noble who lived in the first century B.C. He was infamous for his cruelty. When his slaves displeased him, Pollio had them fed to starving eels—and then he would eat the slave-fattened eels!

Historians believe that eels may have been responsible for ending the siege on Syracuse, Sicily, in 343 B.C. During a break from fighting, the Sicilian defenders and the mercenaries hired by the invading Carthaginian Empire went eel fishing together. The men discovered a shared love of eels, as well as other common values, and they no

A bronze frieze on New York City's Chanin Building shows fish and eels as part of the story of the theory of evolution.

Until the 19th century, people in the United Kingdom believed that eels grew from long, black horsehairs that fell into streams.

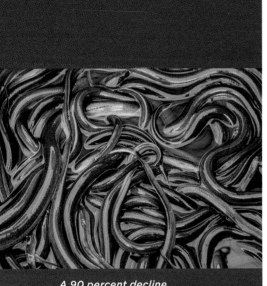

A 90 percent decline in wild freshwater eel populations has turned the Japanese to farmed catfish as a substitute ingredient.

Eels can lay up to 10 million eggs, some as small as pinheads and others as large as popcorn kernels.

longer saw any reason to fight. The mercenaries put down their weapons and went home. Without his hired men to fight for him, the Carthaginian general retreated, leaving Syracuse—and its abundant eels—safely in the hands of the democratic ruler Timoleon.

Strange beliefs about eels persist to this day. Northern Ireland's Lough Neagh, the United Kingdom's largest freshwater lake, is home to the only **commercial** wild eel fishery in Europe. For generations, fishers have trusted in the power of eels to cure ailments. Binding a sore wrist with eel skin is said to ease pain. Some people believe that deafness and earaches can be cured with eel oil. Eels are wrapped in cabbage leaves and placed under hot coals until their bodies are soft. The cooked eels produce oil that is then poured into the ear. Another method is to put an eel in a pot of boiling water for several minutes. As the oil floats to the top of the water, it can be skimmed off and poured into the ear. The cure for baldness is more involved. A person must put an eel in a bottle, cork it tightly, and bury it in a pile of dung for two weeks. The heat generated by the dung will turn the eel to oily mush. Then the person retrieves the bottle and rubs the eel oil

England's River Test is part of a river system used by European eels—and by fishers who set traps for them.

on the scalp. This is believed to make hair grow. Another long-held belief in Ireland was that eating an eel's heart would give a person the ability to see into the future, but eating the whole eel would strike a person speechless.

Fictional beasts popular in tales from Ireland and Scotland were horse-eels, also called kelpies. These creatures were monstrously huge, with the heads and forelegs of horses and the bodies and tails of eels.

FROM THE WATER-BABIES: A FAIRY TALE FOR A LAND-BABY

Tom could hardly stand against the stream, and hid behind a rock. But the trout did not; for out they rushed from among the stones, and began gobbling the beetles and leeches in the most greedy and quarrelsome way, and swimming about with great worms hanging out of their mouths, tugging and kicking to get them away from each other.

And now, by the flashes of the lightning, Tom saw a new sight—all the bottom of the stream alive with great eels, turning and twisting along, all down stream and away. They had been hiding for weeks past in the cracks of the rocks, and in burrows in the mud, and Tom had hardly ever seen them, except now and then at night; but now they were all out, and went hurrying past him so fiercely and wildly that he was quite frightened. And as they hurried past he could hear them say to each other, "We must run, we must run. What a jolly thunderstorm! Down to the sea, down to the sea!"

And then the otter came by with all her brood, twining and sweeping along as fast as the eels themselves; and she spied Tom as she came by, and said: "Now is your time, eft, if you want to see the world. Come along, children, never mind those nasty eels: we shall breakfast on salmon tomorrow. Down to the sea, down to the sea!"

by Charles Kingsley (1819–75)

If disturbed, kelpies were believed to drag a person underwater. Some historians think that the legendary beast was created as a warning to children to stay away from deep water. The kelpie might also be the origin of the Loch Ness monster, a creature said to live in Loch Ness, the second-largest and second-deepest lake in Scotland.

Legendary and mysterious, eels are also historically important. In the early 17th century, eels played a part in the founding of America. When the *Mayflower* landed in the New World in November 1620, the Pilgrims were ill-equipped for hunting and gathering their own food. During their first winter, more than half the immigrants died. The rest were on the verge of starvation. In the spring of 1621, they were saved by eels. Tisquantum, also known as Squanto, was a native of the Patuxet Indians who had spent time in England and spoke English. He served as a translator. One of the first things the Pilgrims learned was how to catch eels. Historians agree that without the teachings of the American Indians and the rich supply of eels, New England's early settlers surely would have died. Historians also note that almost none of today's traditional Thanksgiving foods were on the menu

A myth from Fiji tells of Abaia, a massive eel living on a lakebed that protects the lake's inhabitants from people.

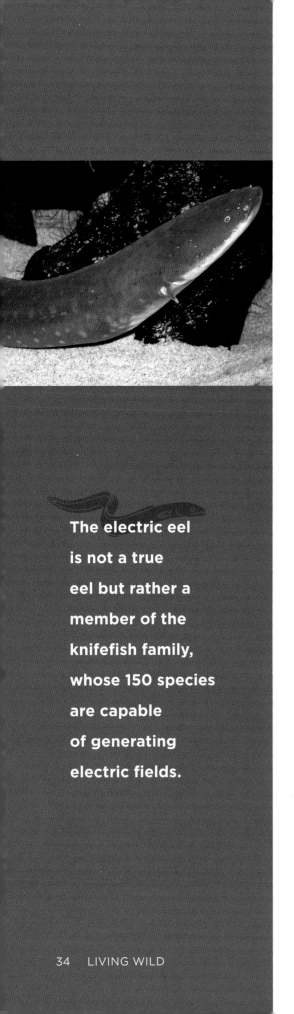

The electric eel is not a true eel but rather a member of the knifefish family, whose 150 species are capable of generating electric fields.

in 1621. Rather, eels were likely the main course, along with mussels, ducks, geese, grapes, plums, and corn.

On the other side of the world, New Zealand's Māori **culture** is infused with the **mythology** of the island's freshwater eels. The Māori were the first humans to arrive in New Zealand about 700 years ago. Freshwater eels became both a staple food and a sacred animal. The Māori word for eel is *tuna* (*TUH-na*). The Māori people believe that the eel is a *kaitiaki* (*KY-tyah-kee*), or guardian. They have long understood the importance of sustainable fishing. Some eels were selected for consumption, while others were treated as family members and regularly fed.

One Māori story tells of Cena, a girl who finds a baby eel and takes it home as a pet. When it grows too big, she sadly releases it into a stream. But the eel loves her, and they continue to play together. One day, a terrible flood comes. The eel uses his body to stop the water and save Cena and her village, but it costs the eel his life. When Cena buries the eel and cries over his grave, a tree springs from the eel's head, becoming the first coconut tree.

In Māori mythology, a *taniwha* (*TAH-nee-fah*) is a shapeshifter that can act as either a protector or a

punisher. In the ocean, taniwha takes the shape of a shark. In the rivers, taniwha is an eel. If people do right, taniwha will watch over them and give them success in fishing and farming. But if people break *tapu*, or a sacred rule, then taniwha will become angry and cause them trouble. One tapu is the killing of an eel that had previously been selected to remain alive. The consequence of this act is *makutu*, which is a curse that will make the offender go insane or die.

On the shore of Lake Taupo, on New Zealand's North Island, a taniwha is depicted as a lizard guarding the lake.

One of the greatest threats to freshwater eel populations is the construction of dams on waterways.

THEY'VE GOT AN EEL BY THE TAIL

While most eels are not in danger of dying out, a number of species are in serious trouble. One of the major culprits is hydropower. Glass eels are able to overcome obstacles such as vertical walls and waterfalls by twisting and braiding their bodies together, literally climbing over each other as they form an "eel ladder." They can reach the top of a smooth concrete dam in this manner. However, once at the top, the eels are frequently chopped to bits by a dam's **turbines**. American freshwater glass eels once flooded into the Mississippi River and its tributaries by the millions as far north as Minnesota. Now, because of hydropower, these eels remain mostly in coastal areas.

The draining of wetlands for agriculture, urban development, and other uses has destroyed freshwater eel habitats. Human expansion has caused many remaining habitats to become polluted with industrial chemicals, pesticides, and wastewater that wreak havoc on fragile glass eels. In addition, scientists are studying how eel spawning, hatching, and larvae development are affected by rising ocean temperatures and shifting currents related to **climate**

The tropical waters off Guam host spawning freshwater eels as well as a variety of resident moray eels.

To spawn, Japanese eels dive into the deepest part of the world's oceans, the Mariana Trench.

Snipe eels, at depths of nearly 2.5 miles (4 km), swim with their mouths open, ready to grab anything that comes near.

change. But perhaps the greatest threat to endangered freshwater eels is human consumption. About 70 percent of all freshwater eels fished in the world are sold to Japan. Called *unagi* in their native land, Japanese freshwater eels were severely overfished, and their population had declined by 90 percent by the 2000s. To satisfy the Asian market, European freshwater glass eels were shipped from Europe to Chinese and Japanese eel farms. This in turn led to a 95 percent decline in the European freshwater eel population. Alarmed, lawmakers put a stop to the trade in 2010. Now only members of the European Union may trade eels with each other, and the sale of eels to Asian countries is prohibited. Despite the law, **poaching** of European eels is rampant. Today, Japan buys American freshwater glass eels. Since the American eel population has also declined by about 90 percent, eel sales are strictly regulated. In 2014, the International Union for Conservation of Nature (IUCN) listed Japanese and American freshwater eels as endangered. The European freshwater eel has been listed as critically endangered since 2008.

Conservationists agree that, in order to protect the future of freshwater eels, people must stop taking glass

eels out of the wild for fish farms. But the secret to sustainably raising eels from larvae has remained elusive. Scientists at Japan's Hokkaido University were among the first to try breeding eels. Eggs from a female eel were artificially fertilized with sperm from a male eel. In 1973, after countless failures, scientists got some eggs to hatch, but the larvae survived only a few days. No one knew that eel larvae eat marine snow, which is dead zooplankton that is being decomposed by special bacteria. Marine snow is impossible to recreate in a laboratory. It

Sushi is made with raw fish, octopus, eel, and other sea creatures combined with seaweed and rice.

Fishing bait gets mature eels to enter traps from which escape usually proves too difficult.

took more than 20 years to formulate a substitute, which is still used today. But this step forward is perhaps two steps back, for the food is made of soy protein and the eggs of spiny dogfish—another endangered species.

Coaxing eels to breed naturally in an artificial habitat has proven impossible. Scientists began giving eels injections of various **hormones** to induce mating. Denmark, Hungary, the Netherlands, and several other European countries as well as Japan use hormones in eel-breeding research. The long-term effects of these hormones are not known because the offspring do not live long. In 2010, for the first time, scientists at Japan's National Research Institute of Aquaculture were able to raise eels from eggs to adulthood. They then induced those eels to produce a second generation of larvae. The survival rate was only 10 percent, but it gave researchers hope. Unless some major breakthroughs occur—or the demand for eels greatly subsides—the future of American, Japanese, and European freshwater eels is limited.

Saltwater eels face their own set of challenges. Because eels do not breed in captivity, many of the more colorful moray species are snatched from their natural habitats to be sold to aquarium enthusiasts. Bright yellow with brown blotches, the dwarf golden moray resembles a ripe banana. It is taken from coral reefs in the Indo-Pacific. The white ribbon eel, also known as the ghost eel, is taken from around Japan's Ryukyu Islands. The black-spotted moray, named for its cheetah-like spots, is taken from western Myanmar. While none of these eels is considered threatened, conservationists are concerned that their absence in the wild could have unforeseen effects on their **ecosystems**.

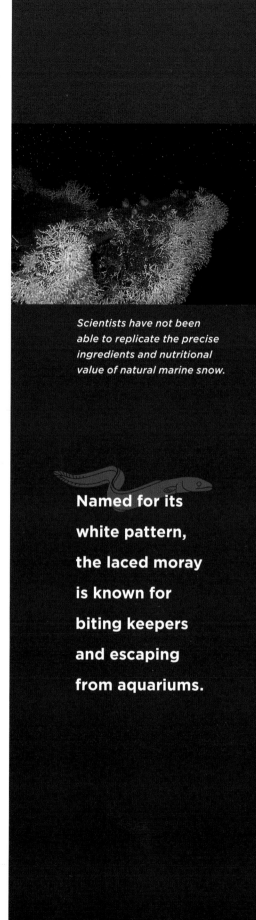

Scientists have not been able to replicate the precise ingredients and nutritional value of natural marine snow.

Named for its white pattern, the laced moray is known for biting keepers and escaping from aquariums.

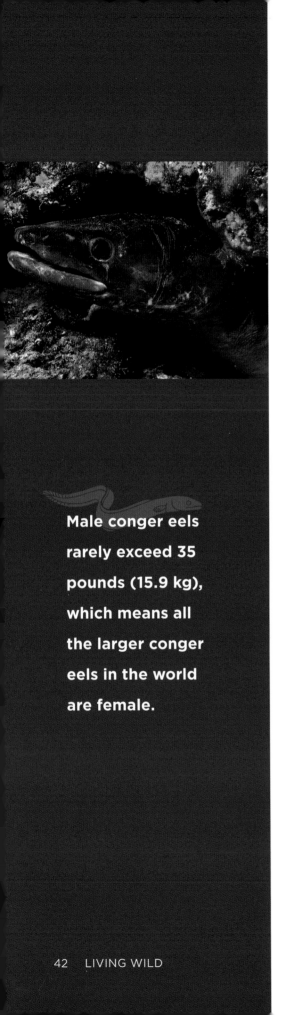

Male conger eels rarely exceed 35 pounds (15.9 kg), which means all the larger conger eels in the world are female.

In 2006, Redouan Bshary, a **behavioral ecologist** from Switzerland's University of Neuchâtel discovered that morays cooperate with groupers. The grouper vigorously shakes its head at the moray, prompting a team hunt. The moray flushes out prey, and the grouper snatches it. Likewise, the grouper chases prey toward the moray. When the prey tries to duck for cover, the waiting moray nabs it. In 2015, biologists from the University of Western Australia published a study on giant morays at Scott Reef. They observed morays tying their bodies in knots to pull food from bait bags and using their tails like paddles to whack food free of containers. Such behavior suggests that morays are important coral reef predators that can hunt and feed in ways that other fish in the ecosystem cannot. Though not endangered, giant morays and other large eel species are targeted by commercial fishermen in parts of Indonesia. Conservationists worry that removing these predators from their coral reef habitats could greatly disturb the **food chain**.

Eels produce slippery mucus that makes holding them with bare hands nearly impossible. The Greek expression "You've got an eel by the tail" means you are pursuing

something that cannot be achieved. Scientists and conservationists may feel as though they've got an eel by the tail when it comes to unlocking the mysteries of these fascinating fish. Freshwater eels likely cannot be saved by captive-breeding, and a clear understanding of the effects of climate change and commercial fishing on elusive ocean-dwelling eels seems out of reach as well. Major advances in technology and research must be achieved if we are to preserve the health of saltwater eels and the very existence of freshwater eels for future generations.

The hunting teamwork exhibited by moray eels and groupers is rare among animals of different species.

ANIMAL TALE: THE EEL PRINCESS

Some of the world's largest moray eels live in the Mediterranean Sea, where Greek fishers sometimes encounter them. This traditional story from ancient Greece features the striking golden-flecked Mediterranean moray eel.

Once upon a time, a king and queen had a son. The prince grew up to be a kind and handsome man. All the ladies of the court wanted to be his princess. One day, while he was walking by the river, he met a maiden fishing for eels. She had soft, olive skin and shimmering, golden hair. Her eyes were deep green. The two talked and laughed. Soon, they fell in love.

The prince asked the maiden to become his wife. She happily agreed. The prince arranged for the maiden to come to the palace. She promised to come the next day. Little did the prince know, a witch had been following him. The witch was cruel and selfish, and she wanted the prince for herself. So the witch hatched a wicked plan.

On her way to the palace the next morning, the maiden was stopped by the witch. The evil woman transformed the maiden into an eel and tossed her into the river. Then the witch assumed the maiden's likeness. She had soft, olive skin and shimmering, golden hair, but her eyes remained dark. *No matter*, she thought, and went to the palace.

The prince had arranged a great feast. His royal fishermen brought buckets of eels from the river. One of the eels flopped out of a bucket and landed at the prince's

feet. It had soft skin and shimmering golden flecks on its dark body. Its eyes were deep green. Something about this eel pleased the prince, and he decided to keep it as a pet. He put it in a silver bowl of water.

The witch, disguised as the maiden, was celebrated and welcomed into the royal family. Weeks passed as wedding plans were made. The prince talked to his pet eel, growing fonder of it every day. This made the witch jealous. When it came time for the wedding, she insisted that the prince kill the eel and serve it to her at their wedding feast. The prince was horrified. He couldn't believe the woman he loved could be so cruel.

The prince refused, which angered the witch. She came at the eel with a knife, ready to slaughter the poor creature herself. She tried to grab the silver bowl from the prince, but his grip held fast. The water in the bowl sloshed about, and the witch, in her blind rage, slipped on the wet floor. She fell on her knife and instantly was transformed into an ugly gray moth that flew away.

With the witch's spell broken, the eel maiden leaped out of the bowl. When she peeled off her eel skin, the prince immediately saw that she was indeed his true love. The eel skin crumbled and turned into a hundred tiny yellow eels—shimmering gold like the maiden's beautiful hair. The prince wed the maiden that day. After the wedding, the prince and his bride released the tiny golden eels into the river. These eels are now Mediterranean morays, which have golden markings on their bodies and deep green eyes.

GLOSSARY

adapt – change to improve its chances of survival in its environment

appendages – parts that project from the main part of the body and have distinct functions

aquatic – living or growing in water

behavioral ecologist – a scientist who studies the effects of environmental pressures on the behavior of animals

captive-breeding – being bred and raised in a place from which escape is not possible

climate change – the gradual increase in Earth's temperature that causes changes in the planet's atmosphere, environments, and long-term weather conditions

commercial – used for business and to gain a profit rather than for personal reasons

crustaceans – animals with no backbone that have a shell covering a soft body

cult – a group of people who worship a particular figure or object

culture – the behaviors and characteristics of a particular group in a society that are similar and accepted as normal by that group

ecosystems – communities of organisms that live together in environments

estuaries – the mouths of large rivers, where the tides (from oceans or seas) meet the streams

food chain – a system in nature in which living things are dependent on each other for food

genetics – relating to genes, the basic physical units of heredity

gullet – the passage by which food passes from the mouth to the stomach

hormones – chemical substances produced in the body that control and regulate the activity of certain cells and organs

larvae – the newly hatched, wormlike form of eels before they become adults

membranes – thin, clear layers of tissue that cover internal organs or developing organisms

mucus – a sticky or slimy substance secreted by glands or organs in a living thing

mythology – a collection of myths, or popular, traditional beliefs or stories that explain how something came to be or that are associated with a person or object

poaching – hunting protected species of wild animals, even though doing so is against the law

turbines – machines that produce energy when wind or water spins through their blades, which are fitted on a wheel or rotor

zooplankton – tiny sea creatures (some microscopic) and the eggs and larvae of larger animals

SELECTED BIBLIOGRAPHY

David, Solomon. "*Anguilla rostrata* – Common Eel." Animal Diversity Web. http://animaldiversity.org/accounts/Anguilla _rostrata/.

"European eel (*Anguilla anguilla*)." ARKive. http://www.arkive .org/european-eel/anguilla-anguilla/.

New Hampshire Public Television. "Muraenidae – Moray Eels." Wildlife Journal Junior. http://www.nhptv.org/wild /Muraenidae.asp.

Prosek, James. *Eels: An Exploration, from New Zealand to the Sargasso, of the World's Most Amazing and Mysterious Fish.* New York: HarperCollins, 2010.

Prosek, James. *The Mystery of Eels.* DVD. New York: PBS, 2013.

Schweid, Richard. *Eel.* London: Reaktion Books, 2009.

Note: Every effort has been made to ensure that any websites listed above were active at the time of publication. However, because of the nature of the Internet, it is impossible to guarantee that these sites will remain active indefinitely or that their contents will not be altered.

The California moray inhabits shallow coastal waters, making it especially vulnerable to pollution and habitat damage.

INDEX